READING THROUGH 'HEBREWS'

Reading Through 'Hebrews'

Six Expository Lectures

BY

R. R. WILLIAMS, D.D.
Bishop of Leicester

LONDON
A. R. MOWBRAY & Co. LIMITED

First published in 1960
Second impression, 1961

PRINTED IN GREAT BRITAIN BY
A. R. MOWBRAY & CO. LIMITED IN THE CITY OF OXFORD
0746

FOREWORD

DURING Lent, 1959, in Leicester Cathedral, I gave six lectures, or 'readings,' in the course of which we (literally) read through the whole of the Epistle to the Hebrews. I delivered them from my *Cathedra*, thus reviving an ancient custom whereby in patristic times authoritative expositions of Scripture were given by bishops from their thrones. This had the advantage that two readers (or lectors) could occupy the chaplains' seats on each side of the throne, and read, as required, the passage of the book next to be expounded.

I now send these lectures out, exactly as they were delivered, as a very minor contribution to the task laid on the Church by the Lambeth Conference (Resolution 12), that of engaging in 'a special effort . . . to extend the scope and deepen the quality of personal and corporate study of the Bible.'

✠ RONALD LEICESTER.

Leicester
Ascensiontide, 1959

CONTENTS

READING THROUGH 'HEBREWS'

1

THE INCARNATION

THE purpose of this course of lectures is to enable us to gain a fuller knowledge of one considerable book of the Bible as a continuous whole. The Epistle to the Hebrews is chosen because its main theme—Priesthood and Sacrifice—is suitable for consideration in the season of Lent, and will lead naturally into Passiontide and Easter. The method will be to have paragraphs read to us; after each reading I shall explain difficulties, draw attention to special points of interest, and show the relevance of the biblical material to our contemporary situation. No special effort will be made to excite popular interest. The course will be demanding of serious application and persevering attention. The reward will come not in the form of immediate emotional elevation, but in the solid edification of our hearts and minds in the deeper truths of our religion.

I shall say little by way of general introduction, for it is the book itself that we want to study.

Hebrews was written at some time before A.D. 96, when it was freely quoted by Clement, writing from Rome. It was written within a circle which regarded itself as made up of second generation Christians, not in the sense that their parents had been Christians, but that they had been evangelized by people who had themselves heard the original proclamation of the Gospel by Jesus Christ.

How shall we escape, if we neglect so great salvation? which having at the first been spoken through the Lord, was confirmed unto us by them that heard; (Heb. 2 [3]).

The readers could look back on persecutions in 'former times,' had not themselves been involved in actual martyrdoms, but were then confronted by testing persecution. They have been described as 'Hebrews' since the third century, but this was probably because of the prominence in the book of contrasts between Judaism and Christianity. They were faced with the temptation to 'apostasize,' to give up their faith, but whether this would have involved a relapse into Judaism, or into other heretical beliefs, it is impossible to say. Recent scholarship has considered it probable that 'Hebrews' was addressed to a group of Jewish Christians in Rome, but this conclusion is far from certain. No one knows who wrote it, and guesses are vain. It was not written by St. Paul, nor does it claim to be so written. In ancient times Eastern Churches thought it was, though Origen never accepted this— 'God only knoweth' was his summary of the dispute about authorship. For a long time it was not accepted as 'canonical' in the west. But Jerome accepted it, and Augustine followed him in doing so.

More important is the main theme of the Epistle. This is summed up in chapter four.

Having then a great high priest, who hath passed through the heavens, Jesus the Son of God, let us hold fast our confession. For we have not a high priest that cannot be touched with the feeling of our infirmities; but one that hath been in all points tempted like as we are, yet without sin. Let us therefore draw near with boldness unto the throne of grace, that we may receive mercy, and may find grace to help us in time of need. (Heb. 4 14-16.)

The message is 'Let us hold fast,' a theme which recurs again and again in the Epistle. The grounds on which this appeal is based are two aspects of one truth. The one truth is the High Priesthood of Jesus Christ—the fact that one has been sent to bring us near to God, and that He has done so. One of the two aspects is His supreme greatness, His unique relation to God, His supremacy over all other mediators, guides, and teachers. The other aspect is His supreme humility, His partnership with us in the trials and tribulations of human flesh. The positive result of holding fast, not letting things slip, is to be seen in drawing near to God, in prayer, in worship, in obedience, in trust. From Him we may find grace to help in time of need. There is little in the whole Epistle which is not comprised in this brief summary.

Now we may turn to chapters one and two, our subject for to-night, which I have described under the main heading of *The Incarnation.*

Let us hear the eloquent words of the opening paragraph familiar to us as the Epistle for Christmas Day.

God, having of old time spoken unto the fathers in the prophets by divers portions and in divers manners, hath

*at the end of these days spoken unto us in his Son, whom
he appointed heir of all things, through whom also he
made the worlds; who being the effulgence of his glory,
and the very image of his substance, and upholding all
things by the word of his power, when he had made
purification of sins, sat down on the right hand of the
Majesty on high; having become by so much better than
the angels, as he hath inherited a more excellent name
than they.* (Heb. 1 [1-4].)

Two approaches of God to man are here contrasted.
One was 'of old time'; one recent, 'at the end of these
days.' One was 'unto the fathers'; one was 'unto us.'
One was in many ways, different forms—'by divers
portions and in divers manners'; one was through a
son, 'one who was pre-eminently Son.' There could
not be a more terse comparison of the Old and New
Testaments.

Having mentioned 'the Son,' the writer appends a
number of great assertions about his work, just as in
the Creed, after the words (I believe) 'in Jesus Christ
His only Son, our Lord' we add the great facts about
His life and work. The Son, says our writer, was
appointed 'heir of all things,' perhaps a reference to
Psalm 2 [8]: 'I will give thee the nations for thine inheritance, and the uttermost parts of the earth for thy
possession.' He is the goal 'to which the whole creation
moves.' Similarly He was the agent through whom the
world was made: 'through whom also He made the
worlds.' Such was His relation to the universe. To
God He was 'effulgence' and 'image'—radiance and
reproduction. Like the beam from a car's headlights,

visible before the car appears, Christ shines with the
light of the invisible God; like the queen's head on a
coin, He reproduces exactly the stamp put upon the
molten metal from the die. In relation to man and his
need He made cleansing or purification for us—by His
Cross—and He sat down at God's right hand—the first
of various references to Psalm 110 [1], 'Sit thou on my
right hand.' The primitive faith about Jesus Christ is
summed up in these words. Christ's position was
unique, and the writer proceeds to show how His
position excelled that of angelic beings. This may not
seem very necessary to us to whom the angels have
become somewhat shadowy figures. It is still necessary
to stress the supremacy of Christ over all other
powers—whether human, like the power of Com-
munism, or natural, like the power of nuclear fission
or malignant cells. He is above all other powers and
potencies.

Now we have a number of quotations from the Old
Testament to illustrate the supremacy of Jesus Christ
to all angelic beings. (Chapter 1 [5-9].)

These are verses which are taken from the Psalms
and other books and are applied by the Church to
Jesus—they bring out the *Sonship* of Jesus Christ.
'Thou art my Son'; 'He shall be my Son.' All the
angels of God are to worship Him—perhaps at His
final coming; perhaps there is a veiled reference to the
chorus of angels singing 'Glory to God' in St. Luke 2.
There always is in mind when I read these words on
Christmas Day! God turns His messengers into winds;
His ministers into flashes of lightning, or so I believe
our author interpreted the words from Psalm 104.

Christ's throne, by contrast, is for ever and ever. The happy anointed Prince of Psalm 45 is taken as foreshadowing the supreme blessedness of the Eternal Son.

Another picture of the changeable contrasted with the eternal is found in Psalm 102, which is now quoted.

And thou, Lord, in the beginning hast laid the foundation of the earth, and the heavens are the works of thy hands; they shall perish; but thou continuest; and they all shall wax old as doth a garment; and as a mantle shalt thou roll them up, as a garment, and they shall be changed; but thou art the same, and thy years shall not fail. But of which of the angels hath he said at any time, Sit thou on my right hand, till I make thine enemies the footstool of thy feet? Are they not all ministering spirits, sent forth to do service for the sake of them that shall inherit salvation? (Heb. 1 [10-14].)

Following the contrast between the outward heavens—grand but temporal—and the Son, whose years shall not fail, the chapter ends with another contrasted pair of pictures—the angels, at best, serving spirits, helping us, the heirs of salvation, and Christ, seated at God's right hand, sharing His sovereign rule over all things.

The next chapter opens with one of the many exhortations to steadfastness—an exhortation based on the supreme authority of the revelation in Christ.

Therefore we ought to give the more earnest heed to the things that were heard, lest haply we drift away from them. For if the word spoken through angels proved steadfast, and every transgression and disobedience re-

*ceived a just recompense of reward; how shall we escape,
if we neglect so great salvation? which having at the first
been spoken through the Lord, was confirmed unto us by
them that heard; God also bearing witness with them,
both by signs and wonders, and by manifold powers, and
by gifts of the Holy Ghost, according to his own will.
(Heb. 2 $^{1-4}$.)*

We must pay most careful attention to the things we
have heard—in the Gospels, in our preparation for
confirmation, in sermons—lest we drift away—are
carried downstream by the tide which runs contrary
to God's Holy Will, the spirit of this world. Lent is an
opportunity to 'give more earnest heed.' The Law was
believed to have been given by angels—by the signs of
wind and fire on Sinai. It proved true enough, as far
as it went. 'Every transgression . . . received a just
recompense and reward.' How can we expect to escape
the due reward of our deeds if we neglect such a
wonderful way of deliverance as has been given us in
the gospel? It rests on a threefold basis of authority.
It was first spoken 'through the Lord'—God spoke in
a Son; the Gospels are the record of it. It was confirmed to us by those who heard—by the apostolic
witness, repeated by the apostolic ministry in every
age. It was sealed as true by accompanying signs—
first the miracles of ancient days, then by every event
which has burned the truth of the message into our
hearts, the *testimonium internum spiritus sancti*, the
inward witness of the Spirit in our consciences.

Now we come to a great passage in which the writer
shows how Jesus has shared our flesh and blood.

B

*For not unto angels did he subject the world to come,
whereof we speak. But one hath somewhere testified,
saying, What is man, that thou art mindful of him? Or
the son of man, that thou visitest him? Thou madest him
a little lower than the angels; Thou crownedst him with
glory and honour, and didst set him over the works of
thy hands; Thou didst put all things in subjection under
his feet. For in that he subjected all things unto him, he
left nothing that is not subject to him. But now we see
not yet all things subjected to him. But we behold him
who hath been made a little lower than the angels, even
Jesus, because of the suffering of death crowned with
glory and honour, that by the grace of God he should
taste death for every man. For it became him, for whom
are all things, and through whom are all things, in
bringing many sons unto glory, to make the author of
their salvation perfect through sufferings. For both he
that sanctifieth and they that are sanctified are all of one:
for which cause he is not ashamed to call them brethren,
saying, I will declare thy name unto my brethren, in the
midst of the congregation will I sing thy praise. And
again, I will put my trust in him. And again, Behold, I
and the children which God hath given me. (Heb. 2* [5-13].)*

The coming age had not been committed to angels,
but to man. Though lower than the angels he was
crowned with glory and honour, all things put under
him. We do not see this happening in our ordinary
experience: atom bombs, cancer, pain and death proclaim the opposite. But there is something we do see.
We see Jesus, standing with the crown of thorns on
His head, destined for the suffering of death. He was

crowned, because by God's gracious will this was no
ordinary death, but death for everyman, for you and
me. The great and beneficent Creator intended to
bring many—all of us—to glory; it was fitting that the
pioneer, the leader in their salvation, the one at the
head of the rope on the mountain, should go to His
perfection through the same hard path of suffering as
all men endured. For the consecrator—Christ—and the
consecrated—us—are both sons of the same God.
So Christ is not ashamed to call us brothers. Quotations from Psalm 22 [22] and Isaiah 8 [17-18] are used to
express Christ's attitude to us: He calls us in one place
brothers, in another 'the children which God has given
him.'

This unity between the Incarnate Christ and us His
people is further developed in the last paragraph of the
chapter.

*Since then the children are sharers in flesh and blood,
he also himself in like manner partook of the same; that
through death he might bring to nought him that had the
power of death, that is, the devil; and might deliver all
them who through fear of death were all their lifetime
subject to bondage. For verily not of angels doth he take
hold, but he taketh hold of the seed of Abraham. Wherefore it behoved him in all things to be made like unto his
brethren, that he might be a merciful and faithful high
priest in things pertaining to God, to make propitiation
for the sins of the people. For in that he himself hath
suffered being tempted, he is able to succour them that
are tempted. (Heb. 2 [14-18].)*

We are involved in a flesh-and-blood situation, with death inevitably before us. The Divine Saviour shared in this situation by His Incarnation. But He shared it in such a way as to transform it. *His* Death was the means of paralysing the evil one who used Death as a means of striking fear and dismay into the hearts of men, those who all their lives live in bondage to the fear of death. He has drawn the sting from death, robbed the grave of its victory.

Yes, in all things He was made like His brothers, like us, so that His qualifications to be our High Priest, standing on the Godward side of us—the well-known translation of the Greek phrase τὰ πρὸς τὸν θεόν—should be complete. He is 'merciful and faithful'—full of sympathy, but utterly reliable. He 'makes propitiation for the sins of the people.' As one of us He goes into God's presence, carrying, as it were, His own precious blood shed for us, a sacrifice sufficient to cleanse and reconcile us all. Having been tempted Himself, He knows what temptation is. He has felt its full force, far more so than we have. Therefore He is able to come to the rescue of those who continue to suffer the trials of temptations. He has suffered; He has been tempted; He has endured; He has overcome. Like the ἀρχηγός, the leader on the mountain expedition, He has overcome the obstacles—He comes down to where we are to lead us over them with His strong hand. Cleansing and strength are thus offered to us.

2

THE GREAT HIGH PRIEST

Wherefore, holy brethren, partakers of a heavenly calling, consider the Apostle and High Priest of our confession, even Jesus; who was faithful to him that appointed him, as also was Moses in all his house. For he hath been counted worthy of more glory than Moses, by so much as he that built the house hath more honour than the house. For every house is builded by some one; but he that built all things is God. And Moses indeed was faithful in all his house as a servant, for a testimony of those things which were afterward to be spoken; but Christ as a son, over his house; whose house are we, if we hold fast our boldness and the glorying of our hope firm unto the end. (Heb. 3 ¹⁻⁶.)

We are described as holy, and as sharers in a heavenly call. This does not mean that we have achieved great moral perfection, but that we have been set apart through having heard God's call to trust and serve Him. We are now summoned to consider 'the Apostle and High Priest of our confession, even Jesus.' The title High Priest will occur again and again and will be considered later. 'Apostle' is an unusual title for our Lord. It means one who is sent, one who is commissioned. In St. John's Gospel Christ repeatedly states that He was sent by God. 'As the Father hath sent me, even so send I you.' The Church is apostolic because it carries on the work of Christ, God's supreme Apostle or 'sent one.' Sent by God as Apostle, He leads us to God as High Priest. The two titles suggest the two-way movement of His Mission, towards man and towards God. Just as the angels ascended and descended on Jacob's Ladder, Christ moves between God and man, bringing both closer together. Then follows a paragraph built around the word 'House.' It arises accidentally, when the writer, having said that Christ was faithful, is reminded of some old words about Moses in Numbers 12 [7], 'he was faithful in all his house,' i.e. as a servant in the midst of God's people, he faithfully fulfilled all his duties towards them. But Jesus was more than a faithful servant. He was a son, sharing His Father's rule *over* the house, which was built by God. We are the House or Family of God, 'if we hold fast.'

The importance of holding fast brings to the author's mind some words which are familiar to us in the *Venite*.

Wherefore, even as the Holy Ghost saith, To-day if ye shall hear his voice, harden not your hearts, as in the provocation, like as in the day of the temptation in the wilderness, wherewith your fathers tempted me by proving me, and saw my works forty years. Wherefore I was displeased with this generation. And said, They do alway err in their heart; but they did not know my ways; as I sware in my wrath, they shall not enter into my rest. Take heed, brethren, lest haply there shall be in any one of you an evil heart of unbelief, in falling away from the living God: but exhort one another day by day, so long

*as it is called to-day; lest any one of you be hardened by
the deceitfulness of sin: for we are become partakers of
Christ, if we hold fast the beginning of our confidence
firm unto the end: while it is said. To-day if ye shall hear
his voice, harden not your hearts, as in the provocation.
For who, when they heard, did provoke? nay, did not all
they that came out of Egypt by Moses? And with whom
was he displeased forty years? was it not with them that
sinned, whose carcases fell in the wilderness? And to
whom sware he that they should not enter into his rest,
but to them that were disobedient? And we see that they
were not able to enter in because of unbelief.* (Heb. 3 [7-19].)

The *Venite* tells of people—the Israelites—who, being
called and delivered out of Egypt, could not thankfully
trust in God, but provoked Him by their disobedience
and lack of trust. Their punishment was not to enter
into the rest which God had prepared for them. The
same doubt confronts us all. We may all 'fall away
from the living God'—drop out of living touch with
Him; cease really to believe in Him. We must empha-
size, to ourselves and to each other, that every day
matters. The challenge is *To-day*—if ye will hear His
voice. The fact that it is still 'called To-day' means that
it is not too late to 'hear His voice.' For our privilege
is great; we are partakers of Christ, but, once more the
writer adds, 'if we hold fast.' For the lesson of the
Old Testament stands sure—it was those who had come
out of Egypt—those who should have been most
grateful—who were provokingly disobedient, and these
were they to whom God had to say 'You shall not enter
into my rest.'

The meditation on the *Venite* continues right down to verse thirteen of chapter four:

Let us fear therefore, lest haply, a promise being left of entering into his rest, any one of you should seem to have come short of it. For indeed we have had good tidings preached unto us even as also they: but the word of hearing did not profit them, because they were not united by faith with them that heard. For we which have believed do enter into that rest; even as he hath said, As I sware in my wrath, they shall not enter into my rest: although the works were finished from the foundation of the world. For he hath said somewhere of the seventh day on this wise, And God rested on the seventh day from all his works; and in this place again, They shall not enter into my rest. Seeing therefore it remaineth that some should enter thereinto, and they to whom the good tidings were before preached failed to enter in because of disobedience, he again defineth a certain day, saying in David, after so long a time, To-day, as it hath been before said, To-day if ye shall hear his voice, harden not your hearts. For if Joshua had given them rest, he would not have spoken afterward of another day. There remaineth therefore a sabbath rest for the people of God. For he that is entered into his rest hath himself also rested from his works, as God did from his. Let us therefore give diligence to enter into that rest, that no man fall after the same example of disobedience. For the word of God is living, and active, and sharper than any two-edged sword, and piercing even to the dividing of soul and spirit, of both joints and marrow, and quick to discern the thoughts and intents of the heart. And there is no creature that is not manifest in his sight: but all things are naked and laid open before the eyes of him with whom we have to do. (Heb. 4 ¹⁻¹³.)

Like the Israelites, we have heard good news: they heard of the promised land; we have heard of the hope of heaven. But the message did them no good. It found no response of faith in the hearers. Faith allows us to enter, here and now, into the promised rest. 'God rested the seventh day,' said the old words. But the people could not share His rest. The *Venite*—long after the days of the wilderness travels—still held out the promise of rest—'To-day—if ye will hear his voice.' Joshua had not been able to give the people rest. So the rest is still available for those who believe. There remaineth—still—a rest for God's people. This is a rest from feverish effort to satisfy God's demands. Our task and privilege is to accept the rest which God offers—'Come unto me,' says Jesus, 'and I will *give* you rest.' To miss this rest through disobedience is serious, for God's words are not to be trifled with. His message is like a living sword, penetrating into our inmost hearts. Nothing is hidden from God's eyes. He knows sin, faithlessness and disobedience for what they are. All things are naked and open before the eyes of Him with whom we have to do.

Now we return to the theme just touched upon at the end of chapter two and the beginning of three— that of Christ as the Great High Priest.

Having then a great high priest, who hath passed through the heavens, Jesus the Son of God, let us hold fast our confession. For we have not a high priest that cannot be touched with the feeling of our infirmities; but one that hath been in all points tempted like as we are, yet without sin. Let us therefore draw near with boldness unto the throne of grace, that we may receive mercy, and may find grace to help us in time of need. (Heb. 4 14-16.)

The supreme reason for holding fast our confession— maintaining our stand as baptized Christians when the Creed first passed our lips, or was said on our behalf— is in the greatness and the approachability of our great High Priest. We *have* a great High Priest, and He has penetrated the heavens. Just as the Jewish High Priest was seen disappearing through the curtains into the Holy of Holies, our High Priest has passed through the heavens, to enter the very presence of God. And our High Priest is not unapproachable. He *can* be touched with sympathetic understanding of our weakness, for He was tempted in every way as we are—sin apart. He was not tempted through His own failures in the past, as we are. But as He never yielded, He felt the full force of temptation as we do not when we yield to its potency. Now then, we must not only 'hold fast,' but 'draw near.' We need not shrink from prayer, from worship, from sacrament. We can approach the mercy seat, the grace-throne. There we shall find mercy— forgiveness for the past. There we shall find 'timely help'—grace for our help just when we need it most.

We now come to one of the great descriptions of our Lord's work as a great High Priest, tender and triumphant.

For every high priest, being taken from among men, is appointed for men in things pertaining to God, that he may offer both gifts and sacrifices for sins: who can bear gently with the ignorant and erring, for that he himself also is compassed with infirmity; and by reason thereof is bound, as for the people, so also for himself, to offer for sins. And no man taketh the honour unto himself, but when he is called of God, even as was Aaron. So Christ also glorified not himself to be made a high priest, but he that spake unto him, Thou art my Son, this day have I begotten thee: as he saith also in another place, Thou art a priest for ever after the order of Melchizedek. Who in the days of his flesh, having offered up prayers and supplications with strong crying and tears unto him that was able to save him from death, and having been heard for his godly fear, though he was a Son, yet learned obedience by the things which he suffered; and having been made perfect, he became unto all them that obey him the author of eternal salvation; named of God a high priest after the order of Melchizedek. (Heb. 5 1-10.)

The writer draws our attention to certain well-known features of human high priests, as known to his readers from the pages of the Old Testament, if not in actual experience at Jerusalem. They are appointed 'in things pertaining to God,' to stand 'on the godward side,' to deal with man's relation to God. They offer gifts and sacrifices for the purpose of expiating or cleansing away sin. They deal gently with sinners, being 'compassed with infirmity' themselves. They have to be called to the work, as Aaron was. With this background sketched in, we are shown how wonderfully Christ fulfils, and more than fulfils, all that is required in a high priest.

He was appointed, so to speak, by God—a fact which the writer illustrates by quoting Psalm 2—'Thou art my son'—and Psalm 110—'Thou art a priest for ever.' These were passages in which the primitive church could not fail to see the life and work of Christ foreshadowed. But how about His identification with suffering and sinful humanity? In a memorable passage, the Epistle shows a clear knowledge of the story of our Lord's Agony in the Garden of Gethsemane. 'In the days of his flesh,' we read, 'he offered up prayers and supplications with strong crying and tears.' We think of the words 'Being in an agony he prayed more earnestly, and his sweat was as it were great drops of blood falling down to the ground.' He prayed 'to him that was able to save him from death.' 'Father, if it be possible, let this cup pass from me.' He was heard for his 'godly fear,' his humble submission. 'Not my will, but thine be done.' 'Though he was a Son'— yes, His prayers were addressed *Abba*, Father, and probably that Aramaic word came into the Christian vocabulary from its use in Gethsemane. He learned obedience—not that He was ever disobedient, but the full meaning of obedience could only be plumbed by obeying. His sufferings took Him into the sphere in which the full reality of obedience revealed itself, and to the abyss from which He cried 'My God, my God, why hast thou forsaken me?' But this led to a perfect achievement, to the *Consummatum est*—'It is finished.' Having been in this sense perfected, He became the source of eternal salvation to those who obey Him, those who commit themselves, body and soul, to His rule and sway. Hence He is thus named by God a High Priest—and next week we shall see what it means that He is further described in the words 'after the order of Melchizedek.'

3

A Priest for Ever

At the end of the last lecture we heard the first reference—there will be many more—to our Lord's status as 'a priest after the order of Melchizedek.' This leads to an interruption of the argument by a passage—three paragraphs long—on the slow rate of spiritual progress made by the readers. Let us hear the first paragraph:

Of whom we have many things to say, and hard of interpretation, seeing ye are become dull of hearing. For when by reason of the time ye ought to be teachers, ye have need again that some one teach you the rudiments of the first principles of the oracles of God; and are become such as have need of milk, and not of solid food. For every one that partaketh of milk is without experience of the word of righteousness; for he is a babe. But solid food is for fullgrown men, even those who by reason of use have their senses exercised to discern good and evil. (Heb. 5 11-14.)

A number of metaphors from physical life and growth are here used to illustrate the slow progress of the readers. The hard things the writer wishes to deal with will not easily be understood, because the readers have grown deaf—dull of hearing. Those who should be teachers need to be taught, and the ABC—the first principles of God's revelation. They need milk: solid

food is beyond them. This latter kind of sustenance is
for men, not babes, for those whose sensitivity has been
developed, who have 'their senses exercised.' How
often those of us who preach and teach are oppressed
by a similar sense that our hearers are not ready for
such deeper teaching as we might wish to give, and this
not because of any intellectual limitation, but because
of a general low level of spiritual vitality and keenness.
For this low level we clergy must bear our share of the
blame. It is for us to exercise—to train and develop—
the spiritual faculties of our people. If they are flabby
and slack, it is partly our fault.

The writer now says that he will leave elementary
principles and press on, and gives a list of the things he
will leave behind. It is this very list of first principles
that is of outstanding interest.

*Wherefore let us cease to speak of the first principles
of Christ, and press on unto perfection; not laying again
a foundation of repentance from dead works, and of faith
toward God, of the teaching of baptisms, and of laying on
of hands, and of resurrection of the dead, and of eternal
judgement. And this will we do, if God permit. For as
touching those who were once enlightened and tasted of
the heavenly gift, and were made partakers of the Holy
Ghost, and tasted the good word of God, and the powers
of the age to come, and then fell away, it is impossible
to renew them again unto repentance; seeing they crucify
to themselves the Son of God afresh, and put him to an
open shame. For the land which hath drunk the rain that
cometh oft upon it, and bringeth forth herbs meet for
them for whose sake it is also tilled, receiveth blessing*

from God: but if it beareth thorns and thistles, it is
rejected and nigh unto a curse; whose end is to be burned.
(Heb. 6 [1-8].)

The 'foundation' contains many of the main points in
our own Catechism and Creed. It begins with repentance and faith, the two pre-requisites for Baptism
according to our Catechism. It goes on to mention
baptism—curiously referred to in the plural—and confirmation under the title 'laying on of hands' (v. 2).
The 'enlightenment' (v. 4) probably means baptism,
which is called the 'illumination' in Justin Martyr.
'Tasting the heavenly gift' suggests First Communion;
'being made partakers of the Holy Ghost' takes us back
to confirmation. 'Tasting the good word of God' shows
us that the primitive church kept the balance between
the Word and the Sacraments, a balance preserved in
the Prayer Book, and being re-emphasized to-day. The
eschatological note is brought in, as in the Creed, in
the words (v. 2) 'the resurrection of the dead and
eternal judgement.'

Those who have experienced all this, and fallen away,
cannot, it is said, be renewed to repentance. This is
always quoted as an example of the 'rigorism' of the
discipline envisaged. Perhaps we should stress the
word 'impossible'—it is not so much that it is for-
bidden, it is inhibited, frustrated. Hardened hearts
cannot be easily softened. But, we may reply, what is
impossible with man is possible with God. The barren
land (v. 8) is 'nigh unto a curse.' But while it is called
'To-day,' the final adverse sentence is not pronounced.

This solemn fate is not one which the writer contem-

plates for his readers—to them, and we trust to us, he
speaks encouraging words.

*But, beloved, we are persuaded better things of you,
and things that accompany salvation, though we thus
speak: for God is not unrighteous to forget your work
and the love which ye shewed toward his name, in that ye
ministered unto the saints, and still do minister. And we
desire that each one of you may shew the same diligence
unto the fullness of hope even to the end: that ye be not
sluggish, but imitators of them who through faith and
patience inherit the promises.* (Heb. 6 $^{9-12}$.)

Obtaining God's promises by faith and patience is
an important theme in this Epistle, and the matter is
opened up in some verses characterized by subtle
argument. Listen to them.

*For when God made promise to Abraham, since he
could swear by none greater, he sware by himself, saying,
Surely blessing I will bless thee, and multiplying I will
multiply thee. And thus, having patiently endured, he
obtained the promise. For men swear by the greater:
and in every dispute of theirs the oath is final for confirmation. Wherein God, being minded to shew more
abundantly unto the heirs of the promise the immutability
of his counsel, interposed with an oath: that by two
immutable things, in which it is impossible for God to
lie, we may have a strong encouragement, who have fled
for refuge to lay hold of the hope set before us; which
we have as an anchor of the soul, a hope both sure and
steadfast and entering into that which is within the veil;
whither as a forerunner Jesus entered for us, having*

C

become a high priest for ever after the order of Mel-chizedek. (Heb. 6 [13-20].)

First God promised great blessing to Abraham; later He 'swore by himself' the same great blessings. He guaranteed the blessing then by a promise and an oath—two immutable things. This guarantee stands for 'the heirs of the promise,' the children of Abraham by faith, the new Israel, that is us, the church of God. Like Abraham, we have laid hold of the hope set before us—the hope we affirm every time we say the Creed. This hope is like an anchor which grips the hidden bed of the sea. Mixing the metaphor, the writer thinks of the hidden heavens, into which our Saviour has already entered—'within the veil.' Christ has gone on before as our forerunner, and He is described once more in the words, now becoming familiar, as a 'High Priest for ever after the order of Melchizedek.'

Now we must be introduced to the original Mel-chizedek.

For this Melchizedek, king of Salem, priest of God Most High, who met Abraham returning from the slaughter of the kings, and blessed him, to whom also Abraham divided a tenth part of all (being first, by interpretation, King of righteousness, and then also King of Salem, which is, King of peace; without father, without mother, without genealogy, having neither beginning of days nor end of life, but made like unto the Son of God), abideth a priest continually. (Heb. 7 [1-3].)

Melchizedek, king of Salem, priest of God most High, is so described in Genesis 14. The name, Melchizedek, means King of Righteousness. His Kingdom 'Salem' means Peace, so he was 'King of righteousness and peace.' Nothing is said in Scripture of his genealogy—he appears, so to speak, 'out of the blue.' We do not read of his birth, or of his death. All this makes him a kind of prototype of our Great High Priest, our Lord and King, source of all our righteousness and peace—he was made like unto the Son of God.

Now listen to another turn in the argument.

Now consider how great this man was, unto whom Abraham, the patriarch, gave a tenth out of the chief spoils. And they indeed of the sons of Levi that receive the priest's office have commandment to take tithes of the people according to the law, that is, of their brethren, though these have come out of the loins of Abraham: but he whose genealogy is not counted from them hath taken tithes of Abraham, and have blessed him that hath the promises. But without any dispute the less is blessed of the better. And here men that die receive tithes; but there one, of whom it is witnessed that he liveth. And, so to say, through Abraham even Levi, who receiveth tithes, hath paid tithes; for he was yet in the loins of his father, when Melchizedek met him. (Heb. 7 4-10.)

In two ways, Melchizedek took up a priestly attitude to Abraham. He blessed him, and he took tithes from him. Abraham was the progenitor of the sons of Levi as of all the tribes of Israel—he was progenitor then of the whole priestly line. Yet when Melchizedek met Abraham, it was Melchizedek who was the priest. Here was a clear sign that there was a higher priesthood than

that of the Jewish line, and of this higher priesthood
we must now learn.

*Now if there was perfection through the Levitical
priesthood (for under it hath the people received the law),
what further need was there that another priest should
arise after the order of Melchizedek, and not be reckoned
after the order of Aaron? For the priesthood being
changed, there is made of necessity a change also of the
law. For he of whom these things are said belongeth to
another tribe, from which no man hath given attendance
at the altar. For it is evident that our Lord hath sprung
out of Judah; as to which tribe Moses spake nothing
concerning priests. And what we say is yet more abundantly evident, if after the likeness of Melchizedek there
ariseth another priest, who hath been made, not after the
law of a carnal commandment, but after the power of an
endless life: for it is witnessed of him, Thou art a priest
for ever after the order of Melchizedek. For there is a
disannulling of a foregoing commandment because of its
weakness and unprofitableness (for the law made nothing
perfect), and a bringing in thereupon of a better hope,
through which we draw nigh unto God. And inasmuch
as it is not without the taking of an oath (for they indeed
have been made priests without an oath; but he with an
oath by him that saith of him, The Lord sware and will
not repent himself, Thou art a priest for ever); by so much
also hath Jesus become the surety of a better covenant.
And they indeed have been made priests many in number,
because that by death they are hindered from continuing:
but he, because he abideth for ever, hath his priesthood
unchangeable. Wherefore also he is able to save to the*

uttermost them that draw near unto God through him, seeing he ever liveth to make intercession for them. (Heb. 7 11-25.)

This long passage is not as difficult as it sounds. The points are really quite clear. A new priesthood—Melchizedek priesthood—had been foreshadowed in the Old Testament. This was a plain hint that there was some inadequacy about the ordinary Levitical priesthood. The writer finds it significant that 'Our Lord sprung out of Judah' (v. 14), i.e. He did not come of the *ordinary* priestly line, which was that of the sons of Levi. And the real difference was that He was not made priest in accordance with a material regulation— a 'carnal commandment'—but because of the irresistible claim of His endless, unconquerable life—'priest *for ever*, after the order of Melchizedek.' Christ belongs to an order of priesthood eternal in character. Of this priesthood there are many partial embodiments in human life. Parents can be priests to their children, officers to their troops, managers and Trade Union officials to employees, parsons to their parishioners. But the one great High Priest—the Priest for ever after this generalized priesthood—is our Lord Himself. Under the old rules there were priests 'many in number,' an endless succession. He lives for ever; His priesthood is unchangeable. Hence He is able to save to the uttermost, completely, finally, those that draw near to God— notice 'draw near' again—through Him. He ever liveth—to make intercession for us. We should not, I think, envisage, even in our mind's eye, the picture of Christ as an eternal supplicant, successively praying for each one of us. The picture is rather that of a High Priest, for ever at God's right hand, interceding for us by what He is, and what He has done for us. Just as Aaron carried on his breastplate the names of the twelve tribes of Israel when he entered the Holy of Holies, so our Lord carries our names, written on His heart, and represents us before God, His perfect humanity and obedience absorbing and cleansing our sinfulness and rebellion.

> Jesus, thy blood and righteousness
> My beauty are, my glorious dress;
> Midst flaming worlds, in these arrayed
> With joy shall I lift up my head.

The chapter ends with the statement that such a High Priest, who could make a 'once-for-all' offering on our behalf, was just what we most needed.

For such a high priest became us, holy, guileless, undefiled, separated from sinners, and made higher than the heavens; who needeth not daily, like those high priests, to offer up sacrifices, first for his own sins, and then for the sins of the people: for this he did once for all, when he offered up himself. For the law appointeth men high priests having infirmity; but the word of the oath, which was after the law, appointeth a Son, perfected for evermore. (Heb. 7 [26-28].)

Chapter eight opens with a summing-up of the argument as far as it has now gone, and begins to prepare the way for the thought of the offering which our Great High Priest offered on our behalf.

Now in the things which we are saying the chief point is this: we have such a high priest, who sat down on the right hand of the throne of the Majesty in the heavens, a minister of the sanctuary, and of the true tabernacle, which the Lord pitched, not man. For every high priest is appointed to offer both gifts and sacrifices: wherefore it is necessary that this high priest also have somewhat to offer. Now if he were on earth, he would not be a priest at all, seeing there are those who offer the gifts according to the law; who serve that which is a copy and shadow of the heavenly things, even as Moses is warned of God when he is about to make the tabernacle: for, See, saith he, that thou make all things according to the pattern that was shewed thee in the mount. But now hath he obtained a ministry the more excellent, by how much also he is the mediator of a better covenant, which hath been enacted upon better promises. (Heb. 8 [1-6].)

Some new thoughts appear at this point. Just as Christ represented a higher priesthood than Aaron's, so the realm in which He ministers infinitely supersedes the earthly Tabernacle or Temple. He is a minister of the true Tabernacle—that spiritual meeting-place between God and man of which the Hebrew tabernacle was but a symbol. Christ's Tabernacle is the one that God pitched—a quotation (Numbers 24 [6], LXX). Moses' tent was admittedly only a copy of a pattern which was heavenly and eternal. Christ brings a better covenant (the 'New Testament'), founded on 'better promises.'

To-night's lecture must end with the writer's treatment of the New Covenant, which consists mostly of a quotation from the Old Testament, from Jeremiah.

For if that first covenant had been faultless, then would no place have been sought for a second. For finding fault with them, he saith, Behold, the days come, saith the Lord, That I will make a new covenant with the house of Israel and with the house of Judah; not according to the covenant that I made with their fathers in the day that I took them by the hand to lead them forth out of the land of Egypt; for they continued not in my covenant, and I regarded them not, saith the Lord. For this is the covenant that I will make with the house of Israel after those days, saith the Lord; I will put my laws into their mind, and on their heart also will I write them: and I will be to them a God, and they shall be to me a people: and they shall not teach every man his fellow-citizen, and every man his brother, saying, Know the Lord: for all shall know me, from the least to the greatest of them. For I will be merciful to their iniquities, and their sins will I remember no more. In that he saith, a new covenant, he hath made the first old. But that which is becoming old and waxeth aged is nigh unto vanishing away. (Heb. 8 [7-13].)

Our writer had seen the tremendous significance of Jeremiah's vision of a new covenant, a new agreement between God and Man. This covenant was to be different from the old agreement made at the first Passover and at Sinai. This time the laws of God were to be written not on tables of stone but on men's minds and hearts. God and His people were to be faithfully bound together. All should 'know the Lord' and men's sins and failure would be swallowed up in God's mercy. This was the New Covenant which Christ instituted at the Last Supper—'This is my blood of the New Covenant.' Once He said 'New,' He had outmoded, out-dated the Old. In any case, as the writer saw, when he looked at Jerusalem threatened by the armies of Rome, the old covenant was becoming old, waxing aged; it was nigh unto vanishing away. Soon it did vanish, and we are the inheritors of the New Covenant. We must beware that we never allow the New Covenant to be so surrounded with material laws and ritual require-ments that its essential newness is tarnished by 'the oldness of the letter.' He hath made the first 'old' when He founded the New. Let us live in 'the newness of the Spirit' and not be entangled again in a yoke of bondage.

4

Eternal Redemption

WE ended last week on the note of the contrast between the Old Covenant and the New. The opening verses of chapter nine look back, perhaps a little nostalgically, to the provision for the worship of God in the first covenant. It is a passage fruitfully compared with St. Paul's words in Romans 9 [3-5]. Speaking of the Israelites, his kinsfolk, he says 'whose is the adoption, and the glory, and the covenants, and the giving of the law, and the service of God, and the promises.' His selection of great distinguishing marks in the old covenant foreshadows the cardinal points of the gospel as he understood it. The writer of Hebrews, by contrast, gives a much fuller picture of *one* category mentioned by Paul, 'the service of God.' Let us hear his description of the 'apparatus' of divine worship based it would seem not on personal reminiscence, but on the instructions for furnishing the Tabernacle in the book of Exodus.

Now even the first covenant had ordinances of divine service, and its sanctuary, a sanctuary of this world. For there was a tabernacle prepared, the first, wherein were the candlestick, and the table, and the shewbread; which is called the Holy place. And after the second veil, the tabernacle which is called the Holy of holies; having a golden censer, and the ark of the covenant overlaid round about with gold, wherein was a golden pot holding the manna, and Aaron's rod that budded, and the tables of the covenant; and above it cherubim of glory overshadowing the mercy-seat; of which things we cannot now speak severally. (Heb. 9 1-5.)

The writer describes the scene affectionately—his own conception of Christianity was largely based on this liturgical aspect of Jewish religion. He shows us the two stages in the approach to God—the Holy Place, a kind of ante-chapel, and the Holiest of all, the Holy of Holies; a kind of innermost shrine. He lingers lovingly over the golden furniture—golden censer or altar, the covenant ark or chest covered with gold, the golden pot with manna. Then there were the cherubim of glory, overshadowing the ark, the lid of which formed the 'mercy-seat.'

We must now hear what went on in this Holy of Holies.

Now these things having been thus prepared, the priests go in continually into the first tabernacle, accomplishing the services; but into the second the high priest alone, once in the year, not without blood, which he offereth for himself, and for the errors of the people: the Holy Ghost this signifying, that the way into the holy place hath not yet been made manifest, while as the first tabernacle is yet standing; which is a parable for the time now present; according to which are offered both gifts and sacrifices that cannot, as touching the conscience, make the worshipper perfect, being only (with meats and drinks and divers washings) carnal ordinances, imposed until a time of reformation. (Heb. 9 6-10.)

The ceremony which the writer specially has in mind is that of the Day of Atonement, a feast-day occurring only once a year. All the priests continually entered the Holy Place in the course of their religious duties. The Holy of Holies, on the other hand, was entered only once in the year; it was entered only by the High Priest; he could enter only when he carried the blood of the sin-offering, which he sprinkled for his own sins, and those of the people. These limitations, when seen against the background of the New Covenant, were a divine way of showing that there was no open access to God for all and sundry. This was a kind of parable the meaning of which became clear in the Gospel period— 'the time now present,' (v. 9)—this parable showed a picture of gifts and sacrifices being offered which could not finally solve the problem of conscience. The gifts and sacrifices were all material in character—outward ordinances consisting of food, drink, ritual worships. They were 'material ordinances'—they could only have been relevant while the day of true revelation in Christ was awaited.

The next section constitutes the Epistle for Passion Sunday. It expresses in pregnant words the nature of Christ's sacrificial offering, compared with all that had gone before.

But Christ having come a high priest of the good things to come, through the greater and more perfect taber-nacle, not made with hands, that is to say, not of this creation, nor yet through the blood of goats and calves, but through his own blood, entered in once for all into the holy place, having obtained eternal redemption. For if the blood of goats and bulls, and the ashes of a heifer sprinkling them that have been defiled, sanctify unto the cleanness of the flesh: how much more shall the blood of Christ, who through the eternal Spirit offered himself without blemish unto God, cleanse your conscience from dead works to serve the living God? (Heb. 9 [11-14].)

'But Christ'—that is the starting-point of an exposition of His High Priestly ministry. He came on to the stage of history a High Priest, not of the old Tabernacle long outmoded, but of the new Tabernacle, that new sphere of relationships between God and man, a realm spiritual in character, 'made without hands,' belonging not to this outward order of creation. The blood which He carried was not animal blood, but His own. He entered Heaven—the Holy Place here mentioned—'once for all.' The deliverance He had won for His people was a final deliverance—'eternal redemption.' Even the blood of animals, properly applied according to the rules of the old covenant, had been effective in cleansing and re-hallowing the Jewish people in respect of their outward ritual defilements. How much more effective must be the sacrificial death, the blood of the Christ, the Messiah. His offering was spontaneous, not involuntary—He offered Himself. Its inspiration was the Eternal Spirit of God, the ultimate source of all action pleasing to God. This offering would work not on bodies but on consciences. It would cleanse them from the deadly influence of sin, and release them for whole-hearted uninhibited service to the Living God.

Now that the writer has broached the subject of the

place in redemption of blood—'life enriched by death'—
he decides to explore this subject further.

*And for this cause he is the mediator of a new covenant,
that a death having taken place for the redemption of the
transgressions that were under the first covenant, they
that have been called may receive the promise of the
eternal inheritance. For where a testament is, there must
of necessity be the death of him that made it. For a
testament is of force where there hath been death for
doth it ever avail while he that made it liveth? Wherefore
even the first covenant hath not been dedicated without
blood. For when every commandment had been spoken
by Moses unto all the people according to the law, he
took the blood of the calves and the goats, with water
and scarlet wool and hyssop, and sprinkled both the book
itself, and all the people, saying, This is the blood of the
covenant which God commanded to you-ward. Moreover
the tabernacle and all the vessels of the ministry he
sprinkled in like manner with the blood. And according
to the law, I may almost say, all things are cleansed with
blood, and apart from shedding of blood there is no
remission.* (Heb. 9 15-22.)

The same Greek word—*diatheke*—stood for covenant, agreement, and testament, a will. Death is
involved before wills become operative. Blood-shed-
ding is necessary before covenants are solemnized. It
seems a *tour-de-force* to us. But here was a fact in
Hebrew religion—almost all things were cleansed by
blood—without shedding of blood was no remission.
Before you dismiss this as purely fanciful, ask yourself
whether ever you knew of healing and restoration

between estranged parties without *someone* carrying a burden of costly love and suffering.

But the things that could be cleansed with outward ceremonies were outward material things. Ultimate spiritual realities—'the heavenly things themselves'— needed another kind of sacrifice, as we shall hear.

It was necessary therefore that the copies of the things in the heavens should be cleansed with these; but the heavenly things themselves with better sacrifices than these. For Christ entered not into a holy place made with hands, like in pattern to the true; but into heaven itself, now to appear before the face of God for us; nor yet that he should offer himself often; as the high priest entereth into the holy place year by year with blood not his own; else must he often have suffered since the foundation of the world: but now once at the end of the ages hath he been manifested to put away sin by the sacrifice of himself. And inasmuch as it is appointed unto men once to die, and after this cometh judgement; so Christ also, having been once offered to bear the sins of many, shall appear a second time, apart from sin, to them that wait for him, unto salvation. (Heb. 9 23-28.)

Once more, and still not for the last time, the writer holds before us the great contrast between the temporary, external ceremonies of the earthly priests and the one eternal, final offering of Christ on the Cross, followed by His entry into heaven. Christ entered no material sanctuary, but heaven itself. The object and nature of this great entrance was 'now to appear before the face of God for us.' It is a wonderful thought. It was one act, a definite self-presentation of humanity as it was intended to be before the eyes of God, but it is eternally contemporary—embraced in the ever-present 'Now.' The whole gospel period is thought of as one present moment—this 'now' is the day of salvation. There can be no repetition of the suffering or of the entrance: he is not to 'offer himself often' (v. 25) nor to suffer often (v. 26). He appeared—in history—at the end of the ages to deal with sin once for all. And what of the future? The writer falls back on a human analogy. Human expectation foresees death, followed by judgment: each man's work will be tried, of what sort it is. Christ, too, has died, but this death is the precursor of another judgement scene—that at which Christ will appear again—like the High Priest returning from the Sanctuary to bring complete salvation to his waiting and expectant church.

The next chapter returns to this contrast between repetitive and final sacrifice, but a new turn is given to the argument, in that stress is laid on the sacrifice of Christ as a sacrifice of willing obedience. A psalm is tellingly used to convey this point.

For the law having a shadow of the good things to come, not the very image of the things, they can never with the same sacrifices year by year, which they offer continually, make perfect them that draw nigh. Else would they not have ceased to be offered, because the worshippers, having been once cleansed, would have had no more conscience of sins? But in those sacrifices there is a remembrance made of sins year by year. For it is impossible that the blood of bulls and goats should take

*away sins. Wherefore when he cometh into the world,
he saith, Sacrifice and offering thou wouldest not, but a
body didst thou prepare for me; in whole burnt offerings
and sacrifices for sin thou hadst no pleasure: Then said
I, Lo, I am come (in the roll of the book it is written of
me) to do thy will, O God. Saying above, Sacrifices and
offerings and whole burnt offerings and sacrifices for sin
thou wouldest not, neither hadst pleasure therein (the
which are offered according to the law), then hath he said,
Lo, I am come to do thy will. He taketh away the first,
that he may establish the second. By which will we have
been sanctified through the offering of the body of Jesus
Christ once for all. (Heb. 10 1-10.)*

The Day of Atonement ceremony was essentially a
'year by year' affair. This itself showed that there was
no final cleansing—the people still had 'conscience of
sins' (v. 2). But our Lord, the true High Priest, could
be thought of as taking on His lips the old words from
Psalm 40: 'In whole burnt offerings and sacrifices for
sin thou hadst no pleasure: Then said I, Lo, I am
come . . . to do thy will, O God.' The writer sees a
sharp contrast between the two forms of sacrifice,
legally ordained ceremonial, and spontaneous personal
obedience. 'He taketh away the first, that he may
establish the second.' The will of God, which Christ
set Himself to do (v. 10) is the ultimate source of our
hallowing 'through the offering of the body of Jesus
Christ once for all.'

Now we come to the last picture of the two priest-
hoods—that of the old covenant and that of the new—
and it is one of the most vivid.

D

And every priest indeed standeth day by day ministering and offering oftentimes the same sacrifices, the which can never take away sins: but he, when he had offered one sacrifice for sins for ever, sat down on the right hand of God; from henceforth expecting till his enemies be made the footstool of his feet. For by one offering he hath perfected for ever them that are sanctified. And the Holy Ghost also beareth witness to us: for after he hath said, This is the covenant that I will make with them after those days, saith the Lord; I will put my laws on their heart, and upon their mind also will I write them; then saith he, And their sins and their iniquities will I remember no more. Now where remission of these is, there is no more offering for sin. (Heb. 10 [11-18].)

You see at once the contrasts. The old priests stood; the great High Priest 'sat down,' because His work was finished. Their sacrifices were repeated daily, but could never deal with sin radically; He offered 'one sacrifice for sins for ever.' All that remained was for His sacrifice to become fully effective and His victory complete—'from henceforth expecting.' So the Holy Spirit, active now, takes up the old words in Jeremiah 31, already quoted in Hebrews 8, about the new covenant, words which end 'Their sins and iniquities will I remember no more.' There is remission now. 'Offering for sin' is over, but we have seen that the presentation of Christ's perfect offering is something that is always contemporary comprised in the immediacy of the eternal 'Now.'

That is really the end of the great theological thesis of the Epistle, viz. that Christ is the supreme, eternal, completely adequate High Priest, able to cleanse, able to save, able to bring us to God, and to the perfection which God has in store for us. A good deal of the rest of the book is in the nature of exhortation, calling on us to avail ourselves of the wonderful opportunities offered. The next paragraph is one such exhortation.

Having therefore, brethren, boldness to enter into the holy place by the blood of Jesus, by the way which he dedicated for us, a new and living way, through the veil, that is to say, his flesh; and having a great priest over the house of God; let us draw near with a true heart in fullness of faith, having our hearts sprinkled from an evil conscience, and our body washed with pure water: let us hold fast the confession of our hope that it waver not; for he is faithful that promised: and let us consider one another to provoke unto love and good works; not forsaking the assembling of ourselves together, as the custom of some is, but exhorting one another; and so much the more, as ye see the day drawing nigh. (Heb. 10 [19-25].)

Those words first summarize the great truths about our position in Christ which have been already established. 'We have boldness to enter the Holy place by the blood of Jesus'—for He has entered that we may follow Him in—one day we shall do so in the whole of our being, now we may 'in heart and mind thither ascend.' The way we must enter in is the way He dedicated, inaugurated, a new and living way, for He is the way. It leads 'through the curtain', through that gap which was opened up when His Body was rent on the Cross, when the veil of the Temple was rent in twain.

And, of course, we *have* a great Priest. Though His sacrifice was in the past, His effective 'Appearance' on our behalf continues in the present. All this being so, what is the call to us?

First, 'let us draw near,' sincerely (with a true heart) believing (in fullness of faith) forgiven (our hearts sprinkled), rejoicing still in our baptism (our bodies washed in pure water). This is what we are called to do at every Holy Communion in the words 'Ye that do truly and earnestly repent . . . draw near with faith and take this holy sacrament.' It is the call that draws us to worship, to private prayer, to identification with Christ in service and obedience.

Secondly, 'let us hold fast'—we have seen before how 'holding fast' goes with 'drawing near.' We have put our faith in one whose promise will not fail.

Thirdly, 'let us consider one another' with a view to deepening the fellowship of the Church. We must not 'forsake the assembling of ourselves together, as the manner of some is'—empty places are no new thing at church services—but we must encourage and help others. The day of final victory draws ever closer. Now is the last time in which to 'slack off.'

Our writer is particularly anxious to leave his readers in no doubt about the serious consequences of deserting Christ and His Church.

For if we sin wilfully after that we have received the knowledge of the truth, there remaineth no more a sacrifice for sins, but a certain fearful expectation of judgement, and a fierceness of fire which shall devour the adversaries. A man that hath set at nought Moses' law dieth without compassion on the word of two or three witnesses: of how much sorer punishment, think ye, shall he be judged worthy, who hath trodden under foot the Son of God, and hath counted the blood of the covenant, wherewith he was sanctified, an unholy thing, and hath done despite unto the Spirit of grace? For we know him that said, Vengeance belongeth unto me, I will recompense. And again, The Lord shall judge his people. It is a fearful thing to fall into the hands of the living God. (Heb. 10 26-31.)

At first sight these words seem to rule out forgiveness for all deliberate sin after baptism, and there have been times when they have so interpreted. Certain people in church history postponed baptism till the hour of death lest they should fall under the sentence of passages like this. But I do not believe that is quite what is meant. The writer has in mind the deliberate and wilful rejection of the way of salvation once experienced in Christ. If we reject this—thus 'treading under foot the Son of God,' cheapening the precious blood of our redemption, insulting the Holy Spirit—we are left with no alternative 'sacrifice for sins.' The clearer interpretation must not blunt the solemn warning of the words.

Once more the writer draws back from a severe passage, to assure his readers—and we hope ourselves—that better things are hoped for.

But call to remembrance the former days, in which, after ye were enlightened, ye endured a great conflict of sufferings; partly, being made a gazingstock both by reproaches and afflictions; and partly, becoming par-

takers with them that were so used. For ye both had compassion on them that were in bonds, and took joyfully the spoiling of your possessions knowing that ye yourselves have a better possession and an abiding one. Cast not away therefore your boldness, which hath great recompense of reward. For ye have need of patience, that, having done the will of God, ye may receive the promise. For yet a very little while, He that cometh shall come, and shall not tarry. But my righteous one shall live by faith: and if he shrink back, my soul hath no pleasure in him. But we are not of them that shrink back unto perdition; but of them that have faith unto the saving of the soul. (Heb. 10 [32-39].)

The readers had borne their share of persecution—when and where we do not know—perhaps in Rome under Claudius. Now the call is for continuance, for patience. How well I know, as Bishop, the truth of this, for if even half of those I confirm were faithful, our churches would be too small for the worshippers. Life seems long in prospect for the young, and perseverance to the end too great an effort. But we must ever remember the danger of slipping back—it leads to 'perdition'—and remember also the reward of faithfulness, the salvation, perfection, and deliverance of our souls.

5

THE CLOUD OF WITNESSES

AT the end of chapter ten, in the course of an exhortation to loyal endurance, the author stressed the importance of faith—the just, he says, quoting Habakkuk, shall live by faith. But what is faith? Hebrews has a special meaning for faith—it is living on the basis that unseen things are desperately real, and must be the real guide in life. In Hebrews 11, the writer lays down this thesis, in a famous verse, and proceeds to illustrate it by a lightning survey of the heroes of the Old Testament. Each case is illuminated by some brief comment, showing how the old stories illustrated the true nature of faith.

Now faith is the assurance of things hoped for, the proving of things not seen. For therein the elders had witness borne to them. By faith we understand that the worlds have been framed by the word of God, so that what is seen hath not been made out of things which do appear. By faith Abel offered unto God a more excellent sacrifice than Cain, through which he had witness borne to him that he was righteous, God bearing witness in respect of his gifts: and through it he being dead yet speaketh. By faith Enoch was translated that he should not see death; and he was not found, because God translated him: for before his translation he hath had witness borne to him that he had been well-pleasing unto

God: and without faith it is impossible to be well-pleasing unto him: for he that cometh to God must believe that he is, and that he is a rewarder of them that seek after him. By faith Noah, being warned of God concerning things not seen as yet, moved with godly fear, prepared an ark to the saving of his house; through which he condemned the world, and became heir of the righteousness which is according to faith. (Heb. 11 ¹⁻⁷.)

Faith is the solid, present reality of things that are still in one sense only hoped for; the establishment as valid of things which cannot be seen by unbelieving eyes. It was to bring out this quality of faith that the Old Testament heroes 'had witness borne to them,' that is, were recorded on the pages of the Old Testament. The writer could not have the Old Testament in book form—only in parchment rolls, but had he had a book, we can imagine him starting at Genesis 1, and skimming through to Malachi, or the Apocrypha.

What of creation? Here the faith has to be shown by us the readers. By faith we understand that the worlds were created by the will or word of God, out of nothing. Science can neither prove or disprove this. We say in the Creed, 'I *believe* in God the Father almighty, *Maker* of heaven and earth.' It is a matter of faith.

An early contrast between two attitudes of mind is that between Cain and Abel. The case is not one of the most obvious, indeed, it is rather difficult to explain. But the point seems to be that Abel entered more generously, more perceptively, into the mind and will of God, and hence stands in sacred record as righteous, because of his obedient faith. Enoch's direct acceptance into the eternal world, without passing through the grave and gate of death, followed from the fact that he pleased God—'he walked with God,' according to Genesis. But 'without faith it is impossible to please Him.' Therefore Enoch is an example of faith. He that cometh to God—and this is true for us—must believe 'that He is,' that He is a reality and, more important, that He is a rewarder, that is, that He is an active force in the changing circumstances of our own lives. This is faith.

Noah is a plain example of what the writer wants to establish. He was warned of the coming flood. Most people ignored the warning, but he set about building an ark. In this way he stepped into the procession, going down all the ages, of those who walk by faith and not by sight.

Now we come to a famous case, that of Abraham and his family.

By faith Abraham, when he was called, obeyed to go out unto a place which he was to receive for an inheritance; and he went out, not knowing whither he went. By faith he became a sojourner in the land of promise, as in a land not his own, dwelling in tents, with Isaac and Jacob, the heirs with him of the same promise: for he looked for the city which hath the foundations, whose builder and maker is God. By faith even Sarah herself received power to conceive seed when she was past age, since she counted him faithful who had promised: wherefore also there sprang of one, and him as good as dead, so many as the stars of heaven in multitude, and as the sand, which is by the sea shore, innumerable. (Heb. 11 [8-12].)

Abraham is the classical example of faith in the Old Testament. He 'believed God, and it was counted unto him for righteousness,' as St. Paul is never tired of saying, quoting Genesis. Here it is his certain faith in the apparently uncertain future that is stressed. God called him out from 'Ur of the Chaldees,' to go to a place promised as an inheritance. He went out, 'not knowing whither he went.' His only security was his trust in God. He and his family lived in tents—they were nomads—in 'the land of promise.' His eyes were on a city not yet visible—a city of God's building, on sure foundations. The first embodiment of this hope was to come in the establishment of Jerusalem as a 'City of God'—'Her foundations are upon the holy hills: the Lord loveth the gates of Zion.' But this earthly Jerusalem, was only a foreshadowing of the eternal city of God. The church is another anticipation of the city which God has prepared for them that love Him. We who walk by faith live already as citizens of that heavenly country. Sarah, in our writer's view, shared her husband's faith. Too old by far to hope for a child, by all standards of human expectation, she yet believed in the divine message that she should have a child; she 'counted him faithful that promised.' So—I cannot forebear to quote the glorious words—'there sprang of one, and him as good as dead, so many as the stars of heaven in multitude, and as the sand which is by the sea shore, innumerable.'

In order to make the meaning quite clear, the writer now summarizes the argument as far as it has gone.

These all died in faith, not having received the promises, but having seen them and greeted them from afar, and having confessed that they were strangers and pilgrims on the earth. For they that say such things make it manifest that they are seeking after a country of their own. And if indeed they had been mindful of that country from which they went out, they would have had opportunity to return. But now they desire a better country, that is, a heavenly: wherefore God is not ashamed of them, to be called their God: for he hath prepared for them a city. (Heb. 11 13-16.)

'These all died in faith'—that was the common feature which bound them all together. By the time of their death they had not actually received the promises—they had only 'greeted them from afar.' It is a wonderful picture—perhaps occasioned by the children of Israel travelling for forty years in the wilderness, many of them dying while the promised land was only an unseen goal and reward of their travelling—they 'hailed it from afar.' They freely described themselves as 'strangers and pilgrims.' Now if you call yourself a stranger—'I'm a stranger here,' says someone who cannot tell you the way—you imply that your home is elsewhere. They thus made it clear that their hearts were set on a fatherland, theirs by promise, but not yet in actual fact.

At any time in their pilgrimage they could have returned, retreated to the old matter-of-fact life, no longer controlled by the unrealized hope—they could have 'drawn back,' as we were warned not to in chapter ten. But the fact that they did not, makes it clear that their hope was for something 'better' than anything they had known—a 'heavenly country.' By now the writer has almost forgotten the old examples, and speaks of all those, in every age, who live by faith, including us. God is not ashamed to be called the God of those who live by faith and hope, for their hope is well grounded—He hath prepared for them a city.

Grand and inspiring thoughts. Plato had had some conception of a perfect city laid up in heaven. But it was St. Augustine, who, trained in Platonism, but transformed by biblical thought, saw how this conception of the quest for God's city could be a guiding thought for a whole philosophy of history. His book, *The City of God*, written as an answer to the shock of the sack of Rome by Alaric the Goth, provided the background to the great mediaeval civilization of Christendom, by means of which Christian light and learning illuminated the so-called 'Dark Ages.' But we must not wander too far from Hebrews. Our privilege is to catch something of this burning faith, which moves through the changing scenes of this earthly life, sustained by an undying hope that God has a 'better country' in store for us, where all that is good here will be preserved and transcended in 'the city God hath made.'

Now the writer returns to the procession of heroes of faith, and he has not yet finished with Abraham.

By faith Abraham, being tried, offered up Isaac: yea, he that had gladly received the promises was offering up his only begotten son; even he to whom it was said, In

Isaac shall thy seed be called: accounting that God is able to raise up, even from the dead; from whence he did also in a parable receive him back. By faith Isaac blessed Jacob and Esau, even concerning things to come. By faith Jacob, when he was a dying, blessed each of the sons of Joseph; and worshipped, leaning upon the top of his staff. By faith Joseph, when his end was nigh, made mention of the departure of the children of Israel; and gave commandment concerning his bones. (Heb. 11 [17-22].)

The willingness to sacrifice Isaac, the very boy who held within him the one possibility of the fulfilment of God's promise, was a remarkable example of true faith. Believing in hope, against all hope, Abraham believed that if necessary God could raise the dead. In a kind of way, says the writer, God did so. Isaac was rescued at the very last moment. Jacob and Joseph showed the same trust in God, in imparting to their surviving sons blessings of which there was no actual evidence other than that visible to the eye of faith.

We have now covered the biblical history down to the time of Moses, and his life and work is now surveyed, and the story of Israel's progress from Egypt to the promised land—culminating in the fall of Jericho—brought into the picture.

By faith Moses, when he was born, was hid three months by his parents, because they saw he was a goodly child; and they were not afraid of the king's commandment. By faith Moses, when he was grown up, refused to be called the son of Pharaoh's daughter; choosing rather to be evil entreated with the people of God, than to enjoy the pleasures of sin for a season; accounting the reproach of Christ greater riches than the treasures of Egypt: for he looked unto the recompense of reward. By faith he forsook Egypt, not fearing the wrath of the king: for he endured, as seeing him who is invisible. By faith he kept the passover, and the sprinkling of the blood, that the destroyer of the firstborn should not touch them. By faith they passed through the Red sea as by dry land: which the Egyptians assaying to do were swallowed up. By faith the walls of Jericho fell down, after they had been compassed about for seven days. By faith Rahab the harlot perished not with them that were disobedient, having received the spies with peace. (Heb. 11 23-31.)

Each great moment in the career of Moses is treated as an example of faith. He was the child of faith, surviving because his parents put him in the bulrush ark, in hope that somehow God would save him, a hope not disappointed. He did not cling to his favoured position as adopted son of Pharaoh's daughter; rather he identified himself with his suffering people. He counted 'the reproach of Christ' preferable to the riches of Egypt. What did Moses know of Christ? Nothing, but our writer sees all the heroes of faith, before and after the life of Jesus, as belonging to one great army of those who endure, as seeing Him who is invisible. Faith is the television screen, which brings the distant, unseen image, into the field of immediate vision. Then follow the further crises of Israel's history, the Passover, the exodus, the entry to Jericho.

But the writer cannot go on in so much detail. He must summarize.

And what shall I more say? for the time will fail me if I tell of Gideon, Barak, Samson, Jephthah; of David and Samuel and the prophets: who through faith subdued kingdoms, wrought righteousness, obtained promises, stopped the mouths of lions, quenched the power of fire, escaped the edge of the sword, from weakness were made strong, waxed mighty in war, turned to flight armies of aliens. Women received their dead by a resurrection: and others were tortured, not accepting their deliverance; that they might obtain a better resurrection: and others had trial of mockings and scourgings, yea, moreover of bonds and imprisonment: they were stoned, they were sawn asunder, they were tempted, they were slain with the sword: they went about in sheepskins, in goatskins; being destitute, afflicted, evil entreated (of whom the world was not worthy), wandering in deserts and mountains and caves, and the holes of the earth. And these all, having had witness borne to them through their faith, received not the promise, God having provided some better thing concerning us, that apart from us they should not be made perfect. (Heb. 11 [32-40].)

These verses skim the course of Old Testament history from the time of the Judges to the Maccabean revolt as recorded in the Books of the Maccabees. The important verses are the two final ones—these all . . . received not the promise. Some better thing was in store for them, something that they could not receive apart from us—the full, final revelation in Christ, and the fulfilment of Christian hope, which we, like them, await in faith.

The opening words of chapter twelve bring this great pageant of heroes of faith to a wonderful conclusion.

Therefore let us also, seeing we are compassed about with so great a cloud of witnesses, lay aside every weight, and the sin which doth so easily beset us, and let us run with patience the race that is set before us, looking unto Jesus the author and perfector of our faith, who for the joy that was set before him endured the cross, despising shame, and hath sat down at the right hand of the throne of God. (Heb. 12 [1-2].)

There is every reason for us to run our race with endurance. All around us is 'the cloud of witnesses.' The writer may have begun with the thought of these men and women as existing primarily on the pages of Holy Scripture, but by now he thinks of them as sympathetic and interested spectators around the arena in which we have to run our course. It is one of the chief passages in which the fellowship of the church militant with the church expectant is clearly implied. Inspired then by their example and strengthened by their fellowship, we must strip for our race, laying aside every weight—every hindrance to our spiritual fitness, and that all-too-easily encumbering sin, we have to set ourselves to our conflict, our stretch of the race. All the time we must keep our eyes on the goal, where Jesus stands to welcome us. He is both starter and finisher, pioneer and consummator of our faith. Attached to the mention of His name is a little creed about Him: He endured the Cross, He despised shame: now He has sat down at God's right hand. The joy of re-entering the Father's presence corresponded in His earthly life to our hope of a joyful welcome from our Master—this was 'the joy set before Him.'

We end this lecture by hearing and expounding another exhortation, this time an exhortation to bear patiently with the trials that come upon us.

For consider him that hath endured such gainsaying of sinners against themselves, that ye wax not weary, fainting in your souls. Ye have not yet resisted unto blood, striving against sin: and ye have forgotten the exhortation, which reasoneth with you as with sons. My son, regard not lightly the chastening of the Lord, nor faint when thou art reproved of him: for whom the Lord loveth he chasteneth, and scourgeth every son whom he receiveth. It is for chastening that ye endure; God dealeth with you as with sons; for what son is there whom his father chasteneth not? But if ye are without chastening, whereof all have been made partakers, then are ye bastards, and not sons. Furthermore, we had the fathers of our flesh to chasten us, and we gave them reverence: shall we not much rather be in subjection unto the Father of spirits, and live? For they verily for a few days chastened us as seemed good to them; but he for our profit, that we may be partakers of his holiness. All chastening seemeth for the present to be not joyous, but grievous: yet afterward it yieldeth peaceable fruit unto them that have been exercised thereby, even the fruit of righteousness. Wherefore lift up the hands that hang down, and the palsied knees; and make straight paths for your feet, that that which is lame be not turned out of the way, but rather be healed. (Heb. 12 3-13.)

E

We do not know what particular persecution or trouble had come upon his readers. Perhaps it was some hardship consequent upon the Jewish War of A.D. 67–70, or perhaps it was some direct persecution because of the name of Christ. It is clear that the writer's answer to the problem is to accept the ills and cross-accidents as part of God's fatherly discipline— God is treating us as sons, not washing His hands of us, as though we were mere bastards. We have to accept God's discipline, and be 'exercised' by it. So the final call is lift up the hands that hang down; strengthen the feeble knees; work out a straight and smooth path, so that even the lame and stumbling Christian can make progress, and become established as a pilgrim on the heavenly way.

6

THE NEW COVENANT

THE last section of the Epistle, like the last section of most of St. Paul's Epistles, is largely concerned with the practical outworking, in behaviour and worship, of the great theological truths that have been established in the earlier chapters. But the particular characteristic of Hebrews is to move rapidly from the ethical to the theological, and *vice versa*. So in between sections which deal with very practical matters, occur other passages of sublime eloquence describing once more the rich world of spiritual reality into which Christians have been introduced. Our first section concerns a practical, ethical point.

Follow after peace with all men, and the sanctification without which no man shall see the Lord: looking carefully lest there be any man that falleth short of the grace of God; lest any root of bitterness springing up trouble you, and thereby the many be defiled; lest there be any fornicator, or profane person, as Esau, who for one mess of meat sold his own birthright. For ye know that even when he afterward desired to inherit the blessing, he was rejected (for he found no place of repentance), though he sought it diligently with tears. (Heb. 12 ¹⁴⁻¹⁷.)

We have to picture the problems arising in a primitive Christian community. They are not so very different from the problems of to-day. There are always those tempted to quarrel; those who remain worldly and unconsecrated; those harbouring bitterness, and thus falling short of God's graciousness; the licentious and the profane. The pastors are warned to watch carefully for such lapses, remembering the fate of Esau. He sold his birthright for a mess of pottage—the opposite attitude to that of faith, which scorns the immediate material advantage. Afterwards, when he found he had lost his father's blessing he was distressed, but all his distress could not undo what had been done. The sense of moral realities is always stressed in this book. Sin is always serious and must be treated as such.

One reason for treating the Christian revelation seriously, and heeding its demands, lay in its superiority to the revelation of God at Sinai, where the law and the covenant were given. This was a serious enough matter, as we shall now hear.

For ye are not come unto a mount that might be touched, and that burned with fire, and unto blackness, and darkness, and tempest, and the sound of a trumpet, and the voice of words; which voice they that heard entreated that no word more should be spoken unto them: for they could not endure that which was enjoined, If even a beast touch the mountain, it shall be stoned; and so fearful was the appearance, that Moses said, I exceedingly fear and quake: (12 [18-21].)

This describes what the Christians have *not* encountered—the tangible mountain of Sinai, with its dark clouds, its flashing lightning and its crashing thunder;

its solemn warnings and the terrifying sentences attaching to disobedience to God's ancient laws. That was solemn enough, but listen to the solemnities attaching to *our* religion.

. . . but ye are come unto mount Zion, and unto the city of the living God, the heavenly Jerusalem, and to innumerable hosts of angels, to the general assembly and church of the first-born who are enrolled in heaven, and to God the Judge of all, and to the spirits of just men made perfect, and to Jesus the mediator of a new covenant, and to the blood of sprinkling that speaketh better than that of Abel. (Heb. 12 ²²⁻²⁴.)

That is one of the greatest passages in the New Testament, and to lay hold of it would be a reward for many weeks of study. It is describing our religion, the whole sphere of spiritual realities to which we have been introduced in coming into touch with Christ. We 'are come to Mount Zion'—not to Sinai, with its commandments, but to Zion, the city of the living God, which virtually means the church visible and invisible, the heavenly Jerusalem. Not a place which God visits in awe and terror, but which, by its whole life and constitution, proclaims His will and owns His law. Myriads of angels in festal assembly surround and serve God's city. The immediate reality to which we are joined is 'the church of the first-born,' that assembly of those who are the heirs of God, the joint-heirs with Christ—'heirs through hope,' as we say in the Prayer of Thanksgiving after the Holy Communion. Their names are all enrolled in heaven. But most wonderful of all, we have been brought into the presence of God, the Judge of all, into fellowship with the righteous of all ages, now at last 'made perfect' by receiving the promise long awaited, and into touch with Jesus, the One who has bridged the gulf between God and man by mediating a new covenant, ratified and sealed by the sprinkling of the blood of Jesus on our hearts—by baptism, by faith, by Holy Communion.

> Abel's blood for vengeance
> Pleaded to the skies,
> But the blood of Jesus
> For our pardon cries.

It 'speaks better things than that of Abel.' Solemn, indeed, then is the warning 'See that ye refuse not Him that speaketh.' Some reasons for not refusing now follow.

See that ye refuse not him that speaketh. For if they escaped not, when they refused him that warned them on earth, much more shall not we escape, who turn away from him that warneth from heaven: whose voice then shook the earth: but now he hath promised, saying, Yet once more will I make to tremble not the earth only, but also the heaven. And this word, Yet once more, signifieth the removing of those things that are shaken, as of things that have been made, that those things which are not shaken may remain. Wherefore, receiving a kingdom that cannot be shaken, let us have grace, whereby we may offer service well-pleasing to God with reverence and awe: for our God is a consuming fire. (Heb. 12 [25-29].)

Those who did not heed the ancient warnings did not escape; nor shall we, if we refuse the solemn message of God in Christ. At Sinai, God shook the earth. But in the book of the prophet Haggai was a text: 'Yet once more will I shake not the earth only but also the heaven.' 'Yet once more'—our writer sees in this the promise of one final critical approach to man. This has taken place in the Incarnation and its sequels. Everything that could be shaken has been shaken, and perhaps the writer envisages the early falling of Jerusalem and its Temple. The unshakeable things remain, and chief among them the Kingdom of God, the City of God, unharmed upon the eternal rock. We are the inheritors of this 'Kingdom which cannot be shaken'; let us therefore seek grace, or use the grace we have, so that we may offer to God that service of obedience and praise for which all the service of Tabernacle and Temple were but a preparation. This service must be no casual affair—it must be offered 'with reverence and awe'—for the God of the New Testament is still a consuming fire.

Now we come to another 'practical' section. As we listen to it we can picture some of the moral problems which weighed upon the primitive community. Some of them still weigh on us.

Let love of the brethren continue. Forget not to shew love unto strangers: for thereby some have entertained angels unawares. Remember them that are in bonds, as bound with them; them that are evil entreated, as being yourselves also in the body. Let marriage be had in honour among all, and let the bed be undefiled: for fornicators and adulterers God will judge. Be ye free from the love of money; content with such things as ye have: for himself hath said, I will in no wise fail thee, neither will I in any wise forsake thee. So that with good courage we say, The Lord is my helper; I will not fear: what shall man do unto me? Remember them that had the rule over you, which spake unto you the word of God; and considering the issue of their life, imitate their faith. Jesus Christ is the same yesterday and to-day, yea and for ever. (Heb. 13 [1-8].)

'Love of the brethren,' 'Love unto strangers'—*Philadelphia, philoxenia* (the words make a convenient pair in Greek). These were the first things required—charity and friendship within the church, and extending outside its borders. They are still the distinguishing marks of a mature and sensitive congregation. 'Those in bonds'—the persecuted—are to be remembered, as we should remember, in prayer and sympathy, those who suffer for their faith, behind the Iron Curtain, or in Moslem lands to-day. The sanctity of marriage was felt sufficiently important to receive special mention. Trust in God, and the rejection of 'feverish lust for gain' are enjoined as plainly as in the Sermon on the Mount. The temptation to slackness as a church passes into its second generation can be seen behind the call to remember the faith and witness of those who had previously been their evangelists and pastors. Jesus Christ does not change; He is the same, yesterday, to-day, for ever. His claims are as great now as ever they were. There is no excuse for getting cool in devotion and casual in obedience.

The readers apparently were under some temptation to desert the great simple truths of the gospel, and to revert to some legalistic religion—Jewish or gnostic. The warning against this leads on to a difficult, but highly important passage about the Christian altar.

Be not carried away by divers and strange teachings: for it is good that the heart be stablished by grace; not by meats, wherein they that occupied themselves were not profited. We have an altar, whereof they have no right to eat which serve the tabernacle. For the bodies of those beasts, whose blood is brought into the holy place by the high priest as an offering for sin, are burned without the camp. Wherefore Jesus also, that he might sanctify the people through his own blood, suffered without the gate. Let us therefore go forth unto him without the camp, bearing not here an abiding city, but we seek after the city which is to come. (Heb. 13 [9-14].)

'We have an altar'—how many columns of detailed exegesis have been written on these four words—only two in Greek! The question has always been whether there is, or is not, a plain reference to the Eucharist, and to the Holy Table round which, and in a sense on which, it is celebrated. I have studied most of the well-known commentators, and have come to feel that a great deal depends on what presuppositions the commentator brings to his task. Those whose minds are nourished on the tradition of the Early Fathers of the Church, on the High Anglican divines of the Caroline period, and on the Catholic teaching of the Church of England as it was revived and re-emphasized in the Oxford Movement gladly grasp this passage as a proof that the sacrificial interpretation of the Eucharist has at least this one clear, unmistakable testimony in Holy Scripture. Those whose minds have been more strongly influenced by the Lutheran strain in Christian thought—of which there are many traces in the language of our own Prayer Book and Articles, are quick to see the difficulties in any easy identification between 'the altar' which the writer says we have, and that which we commonly call 'the altar' in our own churches.

It is one of the encouraging tendencies of theological thought in our own day, and in our own church that the battles of long ago are dying down, and that churchmen of quite varying backgrounds are coming to see that they are closer to each other than they thought.

Let us first unravel the rather twisted strands of this particular passage. Christians must not relapse into legalistic Judaism, says the writer, because at the heart of our religion stands an altar, furnished with sacred food. Those whose picture of the way to God is drawn from outworn Jewish sources, those who 'serve the Tabernacle,' have no right to this food, for they are turning from that one perfect and sufficient sacrifice, Christ crucified, which provides the sacrificial food. After all, says the author, the old sin-offering, that which provided the cleansing blood was not eaten at all; it was burned outside the camp. As a sign of the horror of sin, even the carcase that had been in a sense contaminated had to be destroyed. But Jesus had become the one true offering for sin: that was why He had suffered 'without a city wall.' The *altar* then must be that from which Christians derive the blessings of

Christ's sacrificial death. As it is not more sharply defined, the many interpretations of different expositors can all find some justification. The altar can be Christ Himself or Christ's Cross—as St. Thomas Aquinas taught—'that altar is either the Cross of Christ, in which Christ has been slain for us, or Christ Himself, in whom and through whom we offer our prayers.' But when and where are we most closely united to our Lord in His great High Priestly office? Surely at the Eucharist, when we take our stand before God in Him, when in this sense we plead His Sacrifice, and when we partake of His Body and Blood, His very life, given for us. And as the Holy Table stands as the symbolic centre of that action, we can without any injustice to accurate interpretation, include the actual Altar-Table of our service as a concrete embodiment of the Altar which we are here said to possess.

The verses of the well-known Communion hymn, 'Once, only once, and once for all' seem to me to express the essential truth.

> 'One offering, single and complete,'
>   With lips and heart we say;
> But what He never can repeat
>   He shows forth day by day.
>
> His manhood pleads where now it lives
>   On heaven's eternal throne,
> And where in mystic rite He gives
>   Its presence to His own.
>
> And so we show Thy death, O Lord,
>   Till Thou again appear;
> And feel, when we approach Thy Board,
>   We have an altar here.

The last turn in the argument is a call 'to go forth
unto Him without (outside) the camp, bearing His
reproach.' Originally this probably meant 'abandon all
thought of returning to the old religion: throw your lot
in with Christ whatever the circumstances.' It is a call
to us, suitable for this Holy Week. Moses accepted 'the
reproach of Christ' before Jesus ever lived; we must
accept it two thousand years after the earthly life. Let
us accept whatever sacrifice comes to us for Christ's
sake; we need not expect a carefree life; we are pilgrims; our true home lies ahead.

The next few verses have a strongly Eucharistic
flavour.

*Through him then let us offer up a sacrifice of praise
to God continually, that is, the fruit of lips which make
confession to his name. But to do good and to com-
municate forget not: for with such sacrifices God is well
pleased. Obey them that have the rule over you, and
submit to them: for they watch in behalf of your souls,
as they that shall give account; that they may do this
with joy, and not with grief: for this were unprofitable
for you.* (Heb. 13 15-17.)

We are to offer a sacrifice of praise to God continually, the fruit which God desires, our lips being
filled with our testimony to His grace. The whole
church in the New Testament is a priestly body, a royal
priesthood commissioned to proclaim the excellencies
of Him who called us out of darkness into light. Its
whole life is to be a sacrifice—'Present your bodies a
living sacrifice'—and the sacrifice finds its outward,

cultic expression in the church's worship, and most of all in the Eucharist. It is not that we can repeat, or add to, the perfect sacrifice of Christ. That stands complete. Christ is at the right hand of God, having won eternal redemption for us. At the Eucharist, however, we identify ourselves with that perfect offering. At the Eucharist we are 'at Calvary' in the true 'remembrance of His death and passion'; we are also in heaven, seated with Him in the heavenly places. We are 'in Christ,' He in us, and we in Him. To meet the 'successiveness' of our experience we have to repeat the celebration of the Eucharist, but all Eucharists are parts of one great whole, cells that make up the living organism of the Body of Christ, presented to God by its Head, the great High Priest. The 'sacrifice' spills over into self-giving of other kinds, charity to those in need; loyal obedience to those pastors who are sent to 'watch on behalf of our Souls.'

And now the conclusion.

Pray for us: for we are persuaded that we have a good conscience, desiring to live honestly in all things. And I exhort you the more exceedingly to do this, that I may be restored to you the sooner. Now the God of peace, who brought again from the dead, the great shepherd of the sheep with the blood of the eternal covenant, even our Lord Jesus, make you perfect in every good thing to do his will, working in us that which is well-pleasing in his sight, through Jesus Christ; to whom be the glory for ever and ever. Amen. But I exhort you, brethren, bear with the word of exhortation: for I have written unto you in few words. Know ye that our brother Timothy hath been set at liberty; with whom, if he come shortly, I will see you. Salute all them that have the rule over you, and all the saints. They of Italy salute you. Grace be with you all. Amen. (Heb. 13 [18-25].)

I can only touch on the beautiful blessing of verses twenty and twenty-one. It sums up the whole Epistle, and may well sum up our Lent, and set the tone for our Easter. God is the God of peace, whose love has provided the way whereby we can be at peace with Him. When He brought Christ from the dead, He opened the kingdom to us all. He brought Him forth as a great shepherd to lead us, His flock, from earth to heaven. It cost Him His blood, but by that blood an eternal covenant has been set up. Our great hope is to be made perfect in the sense that we are enabled to live lives that are pleasing in His sight. This can only be through Jesus Christ, to whom be the glory for ever and ever.